Souvenirs

New Women's Voices Series, No. 125

poems by

Dee Matthews

Finishing Line Press
Georgetown, Kentucky

Souvenirs

New Women's Voices Series, No. 125

ACKNOWLEDGMENTS

The author wishes to acknowledge the editors of the following publications in
which these poems first appeared, some in different versions:

Avocet, a Journal of Nature Poetry: "In Winters Dark," "Farm Girls #2," "Pasture
Pastoral," "Proclamation"
Cider Press Review: "Farm Girls"
Worcester Review: "Souvenirs"

Publisher: Leah Maines

Editor: Christen Kincaid

Cover Art: Russell Buzzell

Author Photo: Tom Rettig

Cover Design: Elizabeth Maines

Printed in the USA on acid-free paper.
Order online: www.finishinglinepress.com
also available on amazon.com

Author inquiries and mail orders:
Finishing Line Press
P. O. Box 1626
Georgetown, Kentucky 40324
U. S. A.

Table of Contents

*For George and all farmers who gave their children
the gift of farm life*

Souvenirs

I

My father wanted boys; needed help on the farm.
First one, girl; second one, boy.
Third, fourth, fifth and sixth-all girls.
No matter, we were expected to work like boys.
We shoveled shit with the best of them,
lifted fifty pound hay bales, one in each hand.
Grain bags, cement blocks, buckets of water-
no matter, we were not to cry or
show any sign of weakness.
We slopped pigs, lopped off chickens' heads,
pulled the legs of strangling calves out
of the backsides of their mothers.
Planted seed, weeded seed, gathered in at the end.
Crushed, chopped, diced, stewed,
canned, jarred, bundled.
No complaints, no whining, no matter.

Farm Girls

don't know the difference
between a rock and a hard place
it's all rocks and hard places
all sweat and groans
to on one in particular
although the spider knows
when the hand reaches
to brush the web
clear from the face
rats know too as they
scamper away from
the footfalls and
the calf knows the
touch of fingers
on its nose then reaches
gently to suck the softness
thinking *mother, mother, mother*

II

I had a vision once.
To be given just a chance
at raising a prize-winning
calf of my own to show off
my many, many days
of required care and feeding
at the 4-H fair in the fall.
But I got *don't get attached*
was all from my father.
He didn't know I named you Chooch
after what he called me once.
My Chooch won a prize all right,
won a ride in the trailer
to the slaughterhouse for meat.
I didn't know until then that
I had done a blue ribbon job.

Killing the Chickens

Lit cigarette dangled from his lips.

> I waited having run to him
> carrying his green tobacco tin
> and tiny white rolling papers.

Knife skimmed along his thumb.

> I waited for his signal, slight
> nod of the head, scramble and snatch
> a chicken, deliver her to him.

Chicken writhed in the vise of his legs.

> I waited for the knife to glide across
> the neck, iron-blood smell filled my nose,
> the body collapsed after spasms.

Limp form drained blood onto the ground.

> I waited for his signal, slight
> nod of the head, grab the body and
> plunge it into the scalding water.

Inhaled smoke streamed from his mouth.

> I galloped around chasing one
> too fast for my hands, finally
> pounced, cat-like, bird in hand.

The knife skimmed along his thumb.

III

I yearned to be a boy.
Butchered my hair short
to fit up under
my baseball cap
to look more presentable.
Wanted to try out
for Little League–
just   try   out.
Could hit the ball,
catch and throw too
better than any boy.
Would have made the team easily
but wasn't allowed.
All summer wore
a shirt with
Bill stitched on the pocket.

Farm Girls #2

whirl themselves away
flaunt their stuff
in front of the cats
who sit silently
with elsewhere eyes
wait for the dancer
who pirouettes to the
music in her head
executes a pas de chat
tiptoe turn dumps warm
white liquid into the bowl
the audience magically
assembled to lick and lick

IV

This time I didn't know I was stupid
until I overhead the pharmacist spew
something about *dumb farmers*
when I spilled the pennies from inside
my soggy mitten onto his shiny counter
where he had to finger them, one by one,
to make sure I hadn't cheated him
for the cough drops I especially needed
after I wiped snot on my sleeve
sputtered, sneezed and dripped
standing in the slush puddle
I had melted onto his gleaming floor
tramped in from walking
up town in the snow freezing
to get the insult
I always knew was coming.

Pasture Pastoral

At ten years old, I was amused by play in the pasture.
I leaped along the top stones of the wall
ribboned between our field and the Wendemuth farm.
Happy in my child's imagination,
I didn't see the two old brothers
bowed to the sway of the scythe,
sway of the scythe; the long soft grasses
laid down so gently upon the ground,
straight and connected one to the next.
Wedded to their work, no words left their lips,
they labored with careful determination.
Then lifted their heads and gazed in my direction,
paralyzed my heartbeat, exploded a small alarm in my head-
maybe I had done something wrong to disturb them-
not allowed by children when I was a kid.
In unison they gifted me a smile.
Held me in an instant love-at-first-sight bond;
bent their heads to the sweet, sweet swish
of soft grasses genuflecting to the ground.

V

In the neighborhood where I grew up
knick names branded you.
Everyone had one.
They spoke of who and what you were,
some better than others-
Little Lulu, Boom-Boom, Benji
whose real names was Karl.
Mine happened to be Cow-Patty Queenie
because I lived on the farm
and smelled like cow shit they said.
There were other names:
Fat Sheila, Cabbage Head, Prick,
No Account, Good-for-Nothin' Jerk,
Dummy, Dope, Moron, Idiot.
It would take me a long time to rid
the stigma that came with mine.

Farm Girls #3

swear up and down
they're not in love with farm boys
they long for something different
more like Brando more like Dean
a guy with money a guy with swagger
not one tied to the mule with dirt stained
fingers smelling of dung and hay
with a closed mouth tight lipped
no hope stare into resignation
whose history is long work hours little reward
they want a guy with a future
big wallet big car bigger house
a guy with the big city job big city pay
big city attitude who smells good
still the voice in their heads echoes
no, not for you, not for you

VI

We all endured our jobs
doled out by age and ability
none of us too young
to groan against responsibility.
The small and slight up on the truck
to stack the bales precisely.
Older and stronger walked the field
to heave fifty pounders onto the bed
of the slow moving big black Ford.
Back at the barn, the small and slight
scampered to the loft inferno
to suffer the stacking- stifling, dusty
and dry beyond measure.
Tender hands roughed up by the twine,
I'd curse the three days
of just-right-for-cuttin'-hay weather.

Wash

You can't keep nothin' clean.
Can't hide the fact that
your life's not your own-
belongs to cows, pigs, chickens
and cow shit muck everywhere-
belongs to the land.
You can't go to school like that
with cow shit muck stains
on the cuffs of your jeans.
Even if you rub like mad
you can't get it out.
Even if you scrub and scrub
until your fingers bleed,
the blood just adds to the stain.

VII

Four names on the cake.
It's like no birthday at all.
Like a slap in the face
but I have no face.
I'm just one of several
I should be used to it by now.
I'm just number four down the line
not remarkable at all.
Can't I just have
a cake of my own?
NotHappyBirthdayPepayDadCassieDee
blowoutthecandleshurryupthey'remelting
waxonthefrostingquityourpoutingifyou're
goingtocrygotobedCongratulations
When do I get
a cake of my own?

Farm Girls #4

levitate at the crack
of dawn salute
the early morning
with poignant sighs
lament to the air
whose life is it anyway?
pluck the skin
off the bitter blister
of promise sliced free
from the hefty twine
tethered around their hearts

VIII

I didn't feel I was unworthy
until my two best friends
ran up to two other friends
who grabbed two more
and gushed they were invited
to join the Rainbow Girls.
Between the declaration of disbelief
over the queries of are you serious
through the skepticism of are you sure
past the squeals of delight
and nervous giggles
they strolled, arm in arm,
down our high school corridor
looking all to shocked and sanctimonious
when I softly whispered
I wasn't invited.

In Winters Dark

the farmhouse moans
ungodly cold mocks
to rush headlong
into the rise
of bed and body
demands something more
than you believe
you should give;
to tremble against
the room's arctic air
biting, exploding
into lungs that need
to, must inhale;
make plain the
clock's 4:30 am display
damn this is so unfair

IX

I didn't know I was such a willful girl
until you tried once to put
your hand up under my shirt
in the front seat of your pickup
pushing me hard against the
passenger side door the
handle of the window
jabbing into my side;
until you tried then
to glide your hand up my thigh
your fingers first caressing then clutching, tightening
your hard body crushing into mine
pressing, pressing until I
raised my knee to block your hand
to cripple your adolescent hardness
to shatter your conceit.

Maestro

I slide open the creaky barn door
after the trudge through knee-high snow
and my symphony awaits.
Four thirty five, the lowing begun,
I stare down the long line of bony backs
bent and bumped along like the
rise and fall of small mountain ridges.
Hello girls, had a good night I assume?
The cows anticipate grain, fresh hay
and water so cold it might freeze in their bowls.
Heated breath shot out from their noses
will keep it just warm enough.
On down the line puffs of steam, on down the line
create a comforting rhythm of song.
I begin to hum.

X

I was determined
to be one of seven siblings
to earn a college degree
until my guidance counselor
declared *take business classes*
you're not college material
and shattered my dream.
Held my tears
refused to tolerate his words.
Rushed home to my father
who declined to sign any goddamn papers.
Begged, pleaded, demanded, wailed,
No, was all he said.
Worked two jobs, secured a loan.
Needed six years to complete a four year degree.
I showed them.

Proclamation

No Trespassin'
Jane Hansen
Bloomer Springs Road
McGaheysville
Shenandoah Valley
Virginia

I come upon the sign posted on your land, pretty place.
I wonder about you, are you like me?
Born to the land, put in place by
some larger, greater design.
I know you're not shy about doin' a good day's work.
Hell, you work from daylight to nightfall
and then some dependin' on the weather,
the mighty wind and the birthin' of the calf you been expectin'.
I understand you belong to the land.
There's no splittin' apart, no goin' away.
Your garden grows what you need and then some,
for cannin' and preservin' for the winter meals.
All the hay's in the barn, all the wood cut and split- six cord.
I imagine your hands strong, nails cut short, lined with dirt;
skin taut and browned by hours of work in the sun,
palm lines deep with age, defining who you are
and how hard you've worked.
You walk straight with smooth easy stride.

Virginia
Shenandoah Valley
Mc Gaheysville
Bloomer Springs Road
Jane Hansen
No Trespassin'

$\mathbf{D}$ee Matthews was raised one of seven children on a small family farm in central Massachusetts. Her love and respect for the land and nature comes through from her father, paternal grandmother and great-grandmother, all of Mohawk Native American heritage.

Her poems have appeared in *Avocet, a Journal of Nature Poetry, Cider Press Review* and *The Worcester Review*. Dee was awarded Third Place in The Frank O'Hara Poetry Prize judged by Mr. Lloyd Schwartz for her poem "Souvenirs" as well as Honorable Mentions (*Writer's Digest Writing Competition, Pat Schneider Poetry Contest, Patricia Dobler Poetry Award* and *New Millennium Writings 37th Awards*). Her poems have appeared in two separate anthologies (*Little Red Tree International Poetry Prize* and *Mother Nature's Trail*).

Dee is a member of The Worcester County Poetry Association. In her leisure time, she enjoys hiking, kayaking and gardening. She is celebrating her 38th year of teaching Physical Education to public school children and is looking forward to retirement soon.

www.ingramcontent.com/pod-product-compliance
Lightning Source LLC
LaVergne TN
LVHW021128080426
835510LV00021B/3359